Praise for *One of the Nice Ones*

"Veteran theater provocateur Erik Patterson stings once again in *One of the Nice Ones*... Patterson's play is an exemplar of rudeness whose near-surreal vulgarity elicits torrents of laughter from his gobsmacked audience."

—F. Kathleen Foley, *LA Times*

"This world premiere comedy, despite pre-show warnings of crass situations and adult language, turns out to have a delicate heart reminding us we are our brothers' keepers."

—Dany Margolies, *Time Out LA*

"Fast moving entertainment of substance that will keep you laughing and cringing in spite of yourself. Office politics at its worst and we can't stop laughing."

—Suzanne Birrell, *Discover Hollywood*

"Unflinchingly profane, Patterson has brought the language that we all may use from time to time bubbling to excess with twists and turns that keep us guessing and gasping... Highly recommended for those with a skewed sense of humor and a high threshold for the language of Henry Miller or maybe Christopher Durang on acid. It's a shocking and a totally unexpected rush."

—Michael Sheehan, *On Stage Los Angeles*

"Recommended. Scabrously funny... a comedy that deserves to be experienced with its upending twists and turns left undisclosed."

—Deborah Klugman, *Stage Raw*

"This isn't 'feel good' theater, it's essential theater. It asks us to listen differently, to feel deeply, and to reconsider the world around us. It's begging for a difficult empathy for stories and characters we might rather avoid. *One of the Nice Ones* isn't easy or perfect but it is important."

—Anthony Byrnes, *KCRW*

"It is Patterson's mischievous mind and unsanitized wit that makes *One of the Nice Ones* infinitely nicer than the socially damaged characters he has invented."

—Travis Holder, *ArtsInLA*

"Erik Patterson's intense, outrageous and profane *One of the Nice Ones* is black comedy at its very best."

—Paul Myvold, *Theatre Notes*

"Brilliantly witty and detailed script... Gripping tension."

—Gil Kaan, *BroadwayWorld*

"Topsy-turvy satire."

—Bill Raden, *LA Weekly*

"Entertains with original wit and provokes your mind with scheming clarity."

—Eric A. Gordon, *People's World*

"What a winner is this odd and extremely funny *One of The Nice Ones* by Erik Patterson... Bitingly funny, this satire of these masters of manipulation in their dog-eat-dog corporate world works wonders on our funny-bones. You will laugh, even as you cringe at its un-P.C. moments..."

—Dale Reynolds, *Edge Media Network*

One of the
Nice Ones

Plays by Erik Patterson

Tonseisha
Yellow Flesh / Alabaster Rose
Red Light, Green Light
He Asked For It
Sick
I Wanna Hold Your Hand
One of the Nice Ones
Handjob

Books by Erik Patterson

Pop Prompts: 200 Writing Prompts Inspired by Popular Music
Pop Prompts For Swifties: 99 Writing Prompts
Pop Prompts: the '90s
Pop Prompts Showtunes

One of the Nice Ones

by Erik Patterson

Camden High Street Books
2023

One of the Nice Ones is copyright © 2023 by Erik Patterson

One of the Nice Ones is published by Camden High Street Books

All rights reserved. Except for brief passages quoted in newspaper, magazine, radio or television reviews, no part of this book may be reproduced in any form or by any means, electronic or mechanical, including photocopying or recording, or by an information storage and retrieval system, without permission in writing from the publisher.

Professionals and amateurs are hereby warned that this material, being fully protected under the Copyright Laws of the United States of America and all other countries of the Berne and Universal Copyright Conventions, is subject to a royalty. All rights, including but not limited to, professional, amateur, recording, motion picture, recitation, lecturing, public reading, radio and television broadcasting, and the rights of translation into foreign languages, are expressly reserved. Particular emphasis is placed on the question of readings and all uses of this book by educational institutions, permission for which must be secured from the publisher: camdenhighstreetbooks@gmail.com.

Performance Licensing and Royalty Payments. Amateur and professional performance rights to this Play are strictly reserved. No amateur or professional production groups or individuals may perform this Play without obtaining advance written permission. Required royalty fees must be paid every time the Play is performed before any audience, whether or not it is presented for profit and whether or not admission is charged. All licensing requests and inquiries concerning amateur and professional performance rights should be addressed to the author at erik@erikpatterson.org.

If you cannot obtain the rights to "Rainy Days and Mondays," you have permission to replace it with another song that fits the creative needs of your specific production.

Print ISBN: 978-1-7379853-4-1
eBook ISBN: 979-8-9878016-0-4

Library of Congress Control Number: 2023902386

First Paperback Edition, March 2023

Copy editing by Sherry Angel
Cover image by Elise Wilcox

Printed in the United States of America.
Los Angeles, CA
www.erikpatterson.org

PRODUCTION HISTORY

One of the Nice Ones had its world premiere at The Echo Theater Company (Chris Fields, Artistic Director) in Los Angeles on July 16, 2016. It was directed by Chris Fields. The scenic design was by Amanda Knehans, the costume design was by Elena Flores, the lighting design was by Chris Wojcieszyn, the sound design was by Jeff Gardner, the production stage manager was Emily Burst, the fight choreography was by Ahmed Best, the assistant stage manager was Jessie Vane, the casting was by Meg Fister, and it was produced by Chris Fields and Jesse Cannady. The cast was:

TRACY	Rebecca Gray
ROGER	Graham Hamilton
NEAL	Rodney To
COLLEEN/WANDA	Tara Karsian
ROGER (understudy)	Eric Gutierrez

SETTING

An office of a mid-sized company that sells diet products. It could be any office anywhere. The kind of place where nothing matters more than what—and how much—you sell, sell, sell.

CHARACTERS

TRACY, a woman in a wheelchair, any race. She is a shark who smells blood in the water.

ROGER, her boss, a cis straight white male. The epitome of privilege.

NEAL, a co-worker, a man of color. Genuinely nice, honest, good.

COLLEEN/WANDA, a client, a woman of color. Done being nice. Fuck nice.

NOTES

A beat doesn't necessarily mean a pause, but rather a shift in thought.

Words [in brackets] should be thought but not spoken.

SCENE ONE

A woman in a wheelchair, TRACY, sits across from ROGER, a man in a suit. He looks over some notes on his desk for a beat. Tracy finally breaks the silence:

TRACY: I'm nervous.

ROGER: Don't be nervous.

TRACY: But should I be?

ROGER: No, I told you—

TRACY: It's just—I'm sorry, Roger, but you have so much power and I feel like I should've spent the last three months cultivating more of a relationship with you because I need this job. That sounded really desperate, pretend I didn't say that.

ROGER: Tracy—

TRACY: Oh God, I can tell pretending makes you uncomfortable. You're one of those guys who's not good at pretending. You spend all your time in Literal World. I'm sorry if that was rude of me to say. It was only an observation. I do this all the time. I'm sorry. This is a thing that I do. I talk too much and then I apologize too much, and I'm sorry about that too, but it's all because I let my anxiety take control, and—*no, stop that, Tracy.* You know what? I'm going to *choose* not to be nervous. I'm reading a book on self-actualization and I'm halfway through the empowerment chapter? They talk about how our emotions are a choice. It sounds obvious when you say it out loud, but I never thought about emotions that way. I've always thought of emotions as something that happened to us, but we *choose* to be what we are. Being an emotional wreck is a choice. Being happy is a choice. Not being nervous, that can be a choice too. So that's what I'm choosing now. To not be nervous. Just tell me if you're firing me because the answer to that question will determine how well I'm able to succeed at my emotional choice for the day. So if you're firing me—

ROGER: I'm not firing you.

TRACY: —you can skip the formalities and let me know right now—

ROGER: I'm not firing you.

TRACY: —because I'm a big girl, I can take it.

ROGER: Tracy? Tracy, did you hear what I said?

TRACY: No.

ROGER: I'm not firing you.

TRACY: Really?

ROGER: This is just a performance review.

TRACY: But honestly, when is a performance review *just* a performance review?

ROGER: Right now.

TRACY: Because at the retreat, Neal said he heard from Phil that you guys have to make cutbacks, and he said he was telling *me* because new people are always the first to go, and I know my quota's only at 70 percent this month—I know that and I'm going to fix it, because like I said before: I need this job.

ROGER: Did you enjoy the retreat?

TRACY: I did.

ROGER: That's what you should focus on. Everyone here at Tender Form Weight Loss Systems agrees that you brought a lot to the table. A lot of good ideas. You fit in, you were like one of the guys. In fact, I forgot you were new.

TRACY: That's nice of you. But still. If there are cutbacks—

ROGER: We're not making cutbacks—

TRACY: —I have the least seniority. The thing I keep telling myself, though, is how bad it would look for you to fire the disabled girl.

Beat.

ROGER: That's not how I see you.

TRACY: You don't look at me and see my chair?

ROGER: No.

Beat.

TRACY: Oh.

ROGER (*referring to his notes*): So I was looking at Phil's report, and—

TRACY: I just find it a little disingenuous, that's all. I mean, *I* look at me and see my chair. I don't know why you wouldn't. It's just a weird thing for you to say. It's offensive, actually.

ROGER: How so?

TRACY: It's part of who I am. The chair, it's kind of hard to miss, and—for you to cavalierly say you don't see it, to say it doesn't register—don't you hear how dismissive that sounds? It's like telling a black person that you "don't see color." Which, one, is an outright lie, and two, it's a denial of who that person is when they actually are, by definition, colored.

ROGER: I don't think they like being called that.

TRACY: Are you black?

ROGER: No.

TRACY: Then you're missing my point.

ROGER: I have no idea what your point is—

TRACY: You saying that you don't see my chair, it's like—it's like—it's like telling a female coworker that she's just like one of the guys when she knows that's not *quite* true because you spend an inordinate amount of time staring at her breasts.

Beat.

ROGER: Do I?

TRACY: Yes.

Uncomfortable beat.

ROGER: If we could just focus again, this was supposed to be a good review.

TRACY: Was it?

ROGER: It was.

TRACY: I'm sorry. Okay, good, though. Good to know. Let's do this, then.

Beat.

ROGER: Phil's been raving about what a hard worker you are. Despite your quota. He says you've been greatly influential in getting the Tender Form Weight Loss Systems name out into the marketplace, and that your clients have universally positive things to say about you.

TRACY: I work very hard.

ROGER: Wonderful.

TRACY: I am. I'm wonderful.

ROGER: What?

TRACY: I'm sorry, I heard you wrong—

ROGER: Oh.

TRACY: I thought you were calling me wonderful.

ROGER: I said it's wonderful that you're a hard worker.

TRACY: Right—I get the nuance.

Beat.

ROGER: Look, I'm having a hard time moving on with your performance review. The truth is: there *are* going to be cutbacks.

TRACY: Oh.

ROGER: And we *might* have to let you go.

TRACY: You don't know for sure?

ROGER: Things are up in the air at the moment. I'm sorry. That's why I wasn't going to say anything. This is all so premature. But you kept harping on it, and you seemed so worried and vulnerable that I feel bad lying to you. Hopefully it won't happen, so don't worry—

TRACY: "Don't worry?" Have you listened to anything I've said?

ROGER: Yes—

TRACY: Then do you actually think I'm the type of person who cannot worry about something?

ROGER: *Choose* not to worry. Like that book told you.

TRACY: The book doesn't actually work, Roger. It's a bullshit book, with bullshit theories. Fuck. Fuck! I can't believe you're thinking of firing me. And how you—I mean, the way you just dropped it into the conversation like that—after I asked you before—after you lied to me—I can't believe you just...like an afterthought, like "FYI, you might be getting fired."

ROGER: I'm sorry, Tracy.

TRACY: So, what can I do?

ROGER: We should know for sure about the cutbacks by Friday.

TRACY: You're saying I can't do anything? I'm just supposed to wait?

Roger shrugs.

Beat. Then, with conviction...

TRACY: I'll fuck you.

ROGER: What?

TRACY: I'll fuck you if you promise not to fire me.

ROGER: Are you trying to get me in trouble?

TRACY: No. If we're being recorded right now, let the record show I was joking.

ROGER: We're not being recorded.

TRACY: Then I wasn't joking. Let's fuck. I know you've thought about it, you're curious—

ROGER: Tracy—

TRACY: I see how you look at me. You say you don't notice my chair, but I've seen you look at it. I see you look at my breasts. I know what you're thinking. You wonder what's paralyzed, you wonder what works.

ROGER: That's not how—I mean, I wouldn't, uh...

TRACY: But most of all, you wonder if I ever get laid. I do. I get laid all the time. All the necessary parts work. Unless you're into the dead fish thing, in which case, we could try that too...

ROGER: Uh—

TRACY: My therapist says I use humor as a defense mechanism. I think he's an asshole for saying that.

ROGER: Do you?

TRACY: Yes, I think he's an enormous asshole.

ROGER: No, I mean do you use humor as—I mean, which part of all of *that*, that you just [said]—

TRACY: Oh God, Roger, spit it out.

ROGER: Which part of that was a joke?

TRACY: The dead fish thing—*that* was a joke. Fucking is...

> *She runs a finger over the surface of Roger's desk, suggestively.*

...still on the table.

ROGER: When I went through this conversation in my head before you came in, this is not how I imagined it going.

TRACY: You practiced this conversation?

ROGER: I did.

TRACY: That's sweet.

ROGER: I can't tell if you're being condescending or not.

TRACY: It's genuinely sweet.

So are we fucking or not?

ROGER: Just like that—"are we fucking or not" is suddenly the question.

Wow. This is crazy.

TRACY: You've been so cavalier with me, I can't be cavalier back? After you're all: "FYI, you might be getting fired," I can't be like "FYI, let's fuck." Screw that. FYI, let's fuck.

ROGER: I have to think about this for a second. If anyone found out—

TRACY: They won't.

ROGER: You wouldn't tell anyone?

TRACY: No. FYI, I can see the erection in your pants.

ROGER: That's because, FYI, I'm thinking about your pussy right now.

TRACY: Are you?

ROGER: Yes.

TRACY: Good.

ROGER: Listen—

TRACY: Oh, I'm listening.

ROGER: I want to fuck you. I do—

TRACY: Great.

ROGER: What I'm saying is, it's a very tempting offer—but if someone found out...

TRACY: My last boyfriend was a model. He was the most gorgeous thing you've ever seen. His body was sick. Not too hard, not too soft, just right.

ROGER: Why are you telling me this?

TRACY: Because I want you to know that I fuck models. And you're not a model by any stretch of the imagination. You would be lucky to fuck me. That's what I'm saying.

ROGER: Jesus.

TRACY: I'm saying I need this job. I'm saying let me help you help me. I'm saying let's fuck. It's really not that hard to understand.

ROGER: Okay. Yeah, let's do this.

TRACY: When?

ROGER: Now.

TRACY: Don't think just because I'm offering sex that's all I have to offer. I'm offering sex because I know that's what you want. And I'm efficient.

ROGER: I understand.

TRACY: Now pull me out of this chair—

ROGER: Okay—

TRACY: Put me up on your desk—

ROGER: Yes—

TRACY: And give me some job security.

Blackout.

SCENE TWO

Roger's office. Later.

Everything's been shoved off Roger's desk, onto the floor. Tracy lies on the desk, her legs splayed open, her skirt hiked up around her waist.

Tracy watches Roger get dressed, unmoved.

TRACY: Oh my God, your ass.

ROGER: You like my ass?

TRACY: It's like two round, firm cantaloupes. It makes me want to go grocery shopping.

ROGER: You're exaggerating.

TRACY: No, it makes me hungry, I mean it. It makes me want to feast on its suppleness. Pull your pants back down.

ROGER: Why?

TRACY: I want to look at it again. Men don't get objectified enough. I'm objectifying you. All you are is a piece of ass to me, so show me a piece of your ass. Come on, baby, don't be shy.

He drops his pants, shows her his ass.

Oh, he's doing it. Yes, yes, that's the stuff. That's good. Oh God, I want to bite that sweet, supple fruit.

ROGER (*suddenly self-conscious*): I don't have time for this shit.

> *Roger pulls his pants back up, buckles them again.*

TRACY: It's a shame most people don't get to see the best part of you.
ROGER: We should probably get back to work.
TRACY: I can't get off the desk without your help.
ROGER: Oh, sorry—I didn't—
TRACY: It's okay.
ROGER: I forgot—
TRACY: Stop fumbling for words and help me.
ROGER: Right.

> *He lifts her off the desk and back into her chair.*
>
> *They're awkward together.*
>
> *It takes several moments to get Tracy situated.*
>
> *When she's settled back in the chair...*

TRACY: Okay, so here's what's about to happen. I've been reading the employee handbook and it's very clear about interpersonal relationships at work.

ROGER: What do you mean?

TRACY: Intercourse. Sex. This. We're not supposed to do this. And when I tell corporate, they're going to fire you.

ROGER: What the fuck are you talking about?

TRACY: My plan.

ROGER: What plan?

TRACY: To get you fired.

I'm going to call Phil.

ROGER: What the fuck is happening?

TRACY: Tender Form Weight Loss Systems is about to have a scandal on their hands.

ROGER: You said you wouldn't tell anyone.

TRACY: I lied.

ROGER: You can't do that.

TRACY: But I did.

ROGER: No—no—why would you fucking do that?

TRACY: Maybe I was feeling reckless.

ROGER: No, fuck—this isn't happening.

TRACY: You can't cum inside me—on your desk—in your office—and not expect repercussions.

ROGER: I'm not going to let a crazy fucking bitch ruin my life.

TRACY: I don't have to call them.

ROGER: What do you want?

TRACY: Here's the thing, Roger. I need a certain medical procedure that isn't covered by my insurance. It isn't covered by *any* insurance. But I found a doctor in Mexico who's willing to work with me. I need your help getting it covered. Or paying for it. Whichever's easier. You're the boss. I know you can help with this kind of thing.

ROGER: Are you blackmailing me?

TRACY: I would think of it more like motivation. That's what we sell here at Tender Form Weight Loss Systems, isn't it? "Motivation To Be Your Best Self."

Do the right thing and help me out.

That's what I need your Best Self to do.

ROGER: Fuck no, that's bullshit, that's blackmail.

TRACY: I'm sorry you see it that way.

ROGER: I don't fucking do blackmail.

TRACY: You don't exactly have a choice, Roger. Sorry.

Beat. Damn it.

ROGER: Just tell me what the procedure is. Fuck.

TRACY: You'll do this for me?

ROGER: That's not what I said.

TRACY: Roger—

ROGER: Tell me what it is. I'll help if I can.

TRACY: Thank you.

Beat.

I want them to make me a paraplegic.
ROGER: I thought that's what you already were?
TRACY: Well, yes, but—right now it's only a psychological condition—

She stands up.

—and this doctor in Mexico can make what's in my head a reality.

Lights shift.

SCENE THREE

Tracy sits at her desk, wearing a headset.

NEAL, 30s, sits at an adjacent desk, playing with his cell phone.

Tracy makes a phone call.

TRACY (*practicing the name, wrapping her mouth around it*): Jenelle Waterman. Jenelle Waterman. Jenelle, Jenelle, Jenelle.

They pick up.

Hi, is Jenelle Waterman available? Hi Jenelle, this is Tracy from Tender Form Weight Loss Systems, I'm calling because you filled out a survey in one of our mall kiosks—that's right—yes—yes—well, I'm calling because you've won a free consultation.

Beat.

I understand, but if you have two minutes—

Beat.

Is there a better time I can—

But they've hung up.

Shit.

NEAL (*genuinely trying to be helpful*): You're not supposed to let them hang up.

Tracy side-eyes him.

TRACY: Yeah. I know.

She makes another call.

Jennifer Halter. Halter. Jennifer Halter.

They pick up.

Hi, may I speak to Jennifer Halter? This is Tracy from Tender Form Weight Loss Systems, I'm calling because—hello?

(*under her breath*)

Fuck me.

She hangs up.

Tracy looks over at Neal, who's still playing with his phone.

What are you doing?

NEAL: Playing Smart Happy Apple.

TRACY: What's that?

NEAL: It's a game. Set in a future where apples have become sentient, but they're helpless because they don't have limbs. It's your job to keep them smart and happy.

TRACY: That's the stupidest thing I've ever heard.

NEAL: It's a really good game.

TRACY: Have you hit your quota yet this month?

No reply. He's lost in his game.

Neal?

NEAL: Hm?

TRACY: Your quota.

NEAL: Oh. Yeah. I'm at 130 percent.

TRACY: Of course you are.

NEAL: You?

TRACY: Not at 130 percent.

NEAL: Can I give you a tip?

TRACY: I suppose.

NEAL: Don't let them hang up.

TRACY: Great. Thanks.

Neal goes back to his game.

Tracy makes another call.

Colleen Langley. Colleen Langley. Langley. Langley.

They pick up.

Hey, is Colleen Langley there? This is Tracy. She'll know what it's about.

Beat.

Colleen? Hi, I'm Tracy.
No, you don't know me, please don't hang up.
I'm calling from Tender Form Weight Loss Systems, you filled out a survey in one of our mall kiosks. No—I'm not going to make you buy anything, but it's just—they rate my calls based on how long I'm able to keep the potential client on the line and my calls have been shit today—excuse my language, but they have, they've been shit, just: shit, shit, shit. So if you'd stay on the line with me for a minute, it would really help my—you will?
Oh, thank you.
Yes, thank you, Colleen.
We don't need to talk business, we can just chat. You have a really sexy voice, by the way. You must get that all the time.

Excuse me? No, I'm not hitting on you!

Colleen.

Now I'm embarrassed. I just meant it in a woman-to-woman, I-feel-empowered-by-your sexiness kind of way. There's something disarming about it. I'm surprised you don't—

You're welcome, Colleen, what I was trying to say is: I'm surprised you don't see it, or hear it—the inherent sexiness in your voice. It's quite striking.

Can I ask...

Sorry, no, I shouldn't.

No, I said I wouldn't talk work and it's nice to have a moment with someone that's totally pure, in between all of the bullshit—excuse me—of our daily lives.

Beat.

Really?

Okay: I was going to ask:

Do you like yourself?

It's a real question. I'm asking you to get introspective with me for a moment.

Do you like yourself?

Because I'll be honest, Colleen: I've spent most of my life not liking myself.

Were you popular when you were a kid, Colleen?

No?

Me neither. Girls used to torment me. Oh god, they were *relentless*. Did they—

See, I knew you'd get it! Was there one girl in particular? Who was worse than the others?

Uh-huh.

What was her name?

God, she sounds awful, Colleen. I'm so sorry.

I know!

Of course I did. Her name was Elizabeth Hernandez.

I try not to give her power, though. I try to control the things I can control. Which—oh my god. You won't believe this—I'm actually looking at the survey you filled out at our mall kiosk right now—

(*she isn't*)

—and—this is crazy, but—I was born three days before you were. Same year.

Right?

I always thought I'd have my life together by now. Do you have your life together?

Me neither, not really. But I do like myself now, and I can—I'm not trying to sell you on anything here, I'm just—this is just How It Happened For Me:

That sense-of-self came when I discovered Tender Form Weight Loss Systems.

Did you go to school?

Uh-huh. Oh really? An English degree? I'm sorry.

No, I understand—I went to art school and it was the most frustrating experience of my life. Nothing I made ever looked how I wanted to make it look in my head. I'd have this vision of what I wanted on the canvas and I couldn't translate it. I hate to fail, but this was something I simply couldn't do. After that, I was afraid to express myself artistically for years. Then I realized I was working on the wrong canvas. Because Tender Form Weight Loss Systems, it really—this isn't lip service, but—it turned my body into art.

We can do that for you too.

We can make your body look the way you want it to look in your head.

Do you want your body to be art?

Yes, of course you do, we all do.

Do something about your body, Colleen.

Don't waste this opportunity.

Beat.

Exactly.

I'm so glad you feel that way. How about I book you for your introductory session on Thursday at 3?

Wonderful, I'll email you the details.

Please fast for 24 hours prior to your appointment. That's right.

You're making the best choice for your body, Colleen.

She hangs up.

NEAL: Did you really go to art school?
TRACY: Does it matter?
NEAL: Did you sell any product?
TRACY: I didn't let her hang up. Colleen's coming in for a consultation on Thursday at 3.
NEAL: Hm.

What the fuck was that supposed to mean?

TRACY: I'm doing fine.
NEAL: I didn't say you weren't.
TRACY: You didn't say it with words.
NEAL: I didn't say anything.
TRACY: Then what was that sound?
NEAL: What sound?
TRACY: That sound that came out of your mouth.
NEAL: You think I was judging you? With some sort of sound. That came out of my mouth.
TRACY: Yes.
NEAL: I swear it didn't mean anything. So just, you know...*chill*.
TRACY: Chill?

NEAL: Yeah.

TRACY: I have this ex, his name's Nick. He used to tell me to *chill* like that. Exactly like you just did. Whenever I showed the slightest sign of being mildly upset. And it really rubbed me the wrong way. So one time after he told me to *chill*, I let him know how it made me feel.

NEAL: What did you do?

TRACY: Every day for a week I put medical-grade laxatives in his coffee. He shit so much he was hospitalized.

NEAL: That's horrible.

TRACY: Yeah, well, he never told me to chill again, so it worked out. We're still friends. Do you understand me, Neal?

NEAL: Yes.

TRACY: Good.

Oh, and one other thing? I did go to art school.

But I lied about being frustrated.

I lied about not being able to make the things in my head a reality.

I lied about *that*.

Lights shift.

SCENE FOUR

A break room.

Roger and Neal are at the coffee machine, drinking coffee.

ROGER: So we're going at it, right? And I'm in a good groove—you know, *the* groove—
NEAL: Nice, man.
ROGER: —and I'm talking to her, you know, because she likes it when I talk to her, it's one of the things we've discussed in therapy—I never used to talk while I was fucking, but she likes it and we're trying to do the things that the other one likes—like, she finally started sucking my balls, 'cause the therapist told me to tell her what I wanted and I was like, "I want her to suck my balls," and now she's sucking my balls, like it's on the menu now, you know? Which is a real blessing because...*finally*.
NEAL: Yeah, yeah, totally.
ROGER: If she's gonna suck my balls because of therapy, then I can't bitch about therapy anymore because that shit is working—therapy is being good to me—and if she likes talking during sex—if that's what she's into—if she wants to get verbal—then fuck, you know? It's the least I can do. Even if it doesn't come natural—and you'd think it would, right?
NEAL: Right.

ROGER: So, like, we're fucking, we're fucking, and I'm saying things Like, "You're fucking hot," you know, and, "Do you know how fucking hot you are?" You know?

Like, things like that—just:

"Do you know how fucking hot you are, huh?"

NEAL: That's all you're saying?

ROGER: Jesus, Neal, you expect me to tell you every little thing I tell my wife while I'm fucking her? Don't be a pervert.

NEAL: Sorry—

ROGER: Some things are sacred—

NEAL: I get it—

ROGER: So anyway, she's just taking it, you know? Just taking it, taking it, taking it—

NEAL: Like you're really going at it—

ROGER: Exactly—

NEAL: Hardcore fucking.

ROGER: Right. And then it's like—I suddenly realize she hasn't been answering any of my questions, you know? Which is weird because she fucking knows how hot she is. Like, it's not a difficult question and she's not the type of girl who wouldn't answer that question, you know? Like, she's not shy. And that's when I look at her face—

NEAL: Oh God, oh fuck, this sounds bad—

ROGER: It *is* bad. It's really fucking bad.

NEAL: Shit.

ROGER: Right, okay, yeah, so—I look at her face, right?

NEAL: Yeah?

ROGER: And I realize she isn't breathing—

NEAL: Holy fuck.

ROGER: Right?

NEAL: I knew it was gonna be bad—

ROGER: Yeah.

NEAL: She just stopped breathing?

ROGER: No—I mean, that's the thing—I was wrong—but it *looked like* she stopped breathing, you know? For a second. I mean, I was like: holy shit. I had to stop fucking her for a second to check because—I mean, I really thought she was...*you know*? But instead—

Tracy enters.

Roger quickly stops his story as she wheels towards the coffee machine.

TRACY: Don't stop talking because of me.

ROGER: We weren't talking.

TRACY: You were clearly talking.

ROGER: It wasn't important.

TRACY: Finish your story.

ROGER: I was basically done.

TRACY: Come on, Roger. I'm not an idiot. You were telling a story. About some girl who wasn't breathing—

ROGER: It was my wife, actually.

TRACY: I didn't hear all the details.

ROGER: Not some girl—

TRACY: I just want some coffee.

ROGER: Then make coffee.

TRACY: Me making coffee while you stand there acting like I didn't interrupt your little story is a lot more awkward than you finishing your little story, so please—

ROGER: Fine—

TRACY: —finish your little story.

ROGER: Okay—

TRACY: I beg you.

ROGER: I will.

TRACY: Good.

ROGER: Let's see, where was I?

TRACY: You were fucking your wife and she wasn't breathing.

ROGER: No, she was breathing—I *thought* she wasn't, but she was—

> *He stops as he notices Tracy struggling to reach a mug on one of the higher shelves.*
>
> *The men watch. They don't offer to help.*

TRACY: Could someone...?

NEAL: Yeah, sorry, let me—

Neal grabs the mug. Hands it to Tracy. He grabs the handles on her chair and tries to "helpfully" push her to the table. She immediately jerks away from him.

TRACY: Thanks, I'm good, I can get it from here.

She continues preparing her coffee.

Don't mind me, I'm not even listening.
ROGER: Right, so my wife—it turns out—she was asleep. That's why she didn't answer any of my questions. She was fucking asleep—
NEAL: She fell asleep?
ROGER: Deep fucking sleep. REM.
NEAL: Dude. Way harsh.
ROGER: Yeah. Anyway.
TRACY: What happened after you realized she was asleep?
ROGER: Excuse me?
TRACY: When you were fucking her and you realized your wife was asleep. What did you do?
ROGER: I thought you weren't listening.
TRACY: But you can't sit in the break room—you can't sit *next to me* in the break room—and tell a story about the time you raped your wife—
ROGER: Whoa, whoa, whoa—

TRACY: —and not expect me to listen.

ROGER: I didn't rape my wife—

TRACY: What did you do when you were fucking her and realized she was asleep? What did you do?

NEAL: I'd just like to say that I feel very uncomfortable right now.

TRACY: Did you keep fucking her?

ROGER: Yes.

TRACY: You did?

ROGER: Yeah, but—

TRACY: But what?

ROGER: She's my wife.

TRACY: I'm not getting into the intricacies of what rape is with you, or what levels of understanding you and your wife might have with one another, and I'm not judging you—

ROGER: Are you sure about that?

TRACY: I just think you should know that your story sounds really rapey.

ROGER: She was awake when we started—

NEAL: Yeah, you didn't hear the whole story, she was awake at the beginning—

TRACY: Like I said, I'm not in the mood to debate—

ROGER: Good. How are your numbers today?

TRACY: Eighty-seven percent. I just sent you a progress report.

ROGER: And that woman you've been working on since Monday. Has she caved yet?

TRACY: Of course she caved. That's my job, right? Make them cave.

ROGER: Yeah.

TRACY: Well, I made her cave.

ROGER: Great. I'll check my email. Anyway, I have to roll some calls, so—

TRACY: Where did you cum?

NEAL: Jesus.

ROGER: Excuse me?

TRACY: You heard what I said.

ROGER: I don't think I did.

NEAL: I should probably go now.

Tracy's wheelchair is blocking the way out. She doesn't move aside.

TRACY: Hold on, Neal. I'm talking to Roger.

Beat.

Where did you cum? Did you cum inside her? Or...

ROGER: I don't think this is the kind of conversation people should have at work.

NEAL: I agree with Roger.

TRACY: Oh, believe me, I do too. But I didn't start this conversation.

ROGER: You're antagonizing me.

TRACY: It's merely a question.

ROGER: An antagonizing fucking question.

TRACY: You're the one who told the story.

ROGER: I wasn't telling it to you—

TRACY: All I wanted was some coffee and I had to hear your story, so now I want to hear how it ends. So tell me the end, Roger. Where did you cum?

Beat.

ROGER: On her face.

TRACY: Yeah?

ROGER: Yeah.

NEAL: Wow.

TRACY: Sounds fucking hot to me.

Beat.

Neal, can you leave us alone for a minute?

NEAL: Uh, yeah. I was just—I mean, I was already—I'll go.

Neal exits.

TRACY: Have you made any progress?

ROGER: No.

TRACY: So I should call Phil then? That's what you're saying?

ROGER: It's complicated. Do you really think I can just get the insurance company to cover the procedure you want? No. It has to look like something else, it has to look good on paper, it has to look believable.

TRACY: Just do it.

ROGER: Give me some more time.

TRACY: I want an answer by Friday.

ROGER: Look, I know what you have, Tracy. Body Integrity Identity Disorder. It's a psychological disorder in which sufferers feel they would be happier living life as—

TRACY: I KNOW WHAT IT IS.

ROGER: We can get you counseling.

TRACY: I'm way beyond counseling.

ROGER: No, just hear me out—we can end this right now. I found a doctor who specializes in people like you—

TRACY: People like me?

ROGER: You know what I mean.

TRACY: I do, Roger, and I'm not even remotely interested. I've had counseling and it doesn't work. The only thing that works is this doctor in Mexico.

ROGER: Just hear me out—

It's like a punch to Tracy's gut. Emotion suddenly bubbling up to the surface. Anger, fear, sadness, all of it...

TRACY: I have a right to exist the way I feel inside.

ROGER: I'm not saying you don't—

TRACY: I will do whatever I need to do, Roger. You don't want to test me.
ROGER: But if you could get some help—
TRACY: You don't get it, I've gotten help: this is me with help. What I need now is for you to get an answer from corporate so we can end this.
ROGER: Fine. I'll work on it.

> *Tracy tamps down her feelings, quickly getting control of her emotions again.*

TRACY: Great. Now can you grab me some Splenda? We're out down here.
ROGER: Really?

> *Beat.*

We're alone now.
TRACY: So?
ROGER: So you don't need me to grab it for you.
TRACY: Actually I do, Roger.

> *He grabs a Splenda. Hands it to her. She wheels out of the room.*
>
> *Lights shift.*

SCENE FIVE

The Men's Room.

Neal stands at the urinal.

Roger enters and takes the urinal next to him.

NEAL: Hey.

Roger gives him a nod. Lets out a sigh of relief as he pees.

You're lucky, man.

(*off Roger's look*)

That you can just *start* like that. It takes me at least five minutes of standing here before I can get a stream going.
ROGER: You should see a doctor. That sounds like a problem.

Neal glances over at Roger.

Did you just look at my dick?
NEAL: No.

ROGER: Bullshit.

NEAL: I mean, okay, maybe I glanced—

ROGER: Yeah, you did.

NEAL: —but it was more like when you glance in a random direction and something just *happens* to catch your eye—not like I was looking at it on purpose.

ROGER: It just "caught your eye." That's your story?

NEAL: I mean, yeah.

ROGER: Look at it again.

NEAL: Uh, no, thanks.

ROGER: I think you misunderstood me. I wasn't *asking* if you wanted to look at it again. I was telling you.

Beat.

How long have you been working here?

NEAL: About a year and a half.

ROGER: Thirteen months, actually. Me, I've been here for twelve years. As far as seniority goes, you are the shit underneath my shoe. I say that with no disrespect. I say it with love. It's also with love that I'm telling you to take a better look at my cock. Really take it in this time. Got it? Say "yes."

NEAL: Yes.

Roger steps back from the urinal, as Neal looks again.

ROGER: Get a good look?

NEAL (*embarrassed*): Yeah, I saw it.

ROGER: I want you to remember that. Next time you question something I say to you. Remember what I have in my pants.

NEAL: Okay, sure. Fine.

Roger zips up his pants.

ROGER: Now you step back.

NEAL: Huh?

ROGER: Step back from the urinal.

NEAL: Why?

ROGER: You saw mine. Show me yours.

Neal reluctantly takes a step back. Roger looks him over, impressed.

Really?

NEAL: What do you mean "really?"

ROGER: I didn't think it would be that big.

NEAL: Why not?

ROGER: Because you don't act like a guy with a huge dick.

NEAL: How am I supposed to act?

ROGER: Put your cock away. I don't want to look at that thing anymore.

NEAL: I haven't peed yet.

ROGER: And like I said before, you should see a doctor about that. Now zip the fuck up. Come on, man.

Neal zips up his pants.

Do you think you're beautiful?
NEAL: What? Why would I even—
ROGER: It's an easy question.
NEAL: But why would I think that?
ROGER: I'm not asking you this in, like, a gay faggoty fey-fey way. This is a real question. Do you think you're beautiful?

Beat.

NEAL: No.
ROGER: See, that's part of your problem. Because if you want to make it in this business—hell, if you want to make it in life—you've gotta believe you're fucking beautiful.
NEAL: I don't see how that's—
ROGER: I'm gonna give you some personal insight. Are you ready for some personal insight?
NEAL: Okay, I guess—
ROGER: I don't like my nose. I think it's too big.
NEAL: It seems fine to me—
ROGER: Don't interrupt me, I'm not fishing for compliments—just let me finish, I'm trying to make a point here, okay?

NEAL: Sorry—

ROGER: My nose is bigger than it should be. Like it was in the oven too long. It just sits there on my face like a mistake. I used to let it get me down. Then one day I realized I was giving my nose too much power. My nose was holding me back. After all, it's just a fucking nose, right? Let other assholes worry about that shit. I'm gonna own this nose. I'm gonna wear it with pride. Because I'm a unique, fucking beautiful individual. I'm a butterfly. You're a butterfly too. Tell me you're a butterfly.

NEAL: I'm a butterfly?

ROGER: I didn't believe that at all. Have a backbone. Say it again.

NEAL (*still tentative, but a little stronger*): I'm a butterfly.

ROGER: Butterflies don't slouch, they fucking float. They spread their wings and soar. They don't settle for less, they strive for best. Say it again!

NEAL: I'm a butterfly!

ROGER: Better, but I still don't believe it. Do you know why I don't believe it? Because you don't believe it.

NEAL: I know, but—

ROGER: Look, when I started to embrace my physical flaws, people looked at me different. And I don't say that lightly: there was a noticeable, powerful shift in the way people treated me. And like, with you, you have a big-ass cock. But you don't own your big-ass cock. You act like it's some dirty secret, when it should be the source of your power.

NEAL: I just don't think—

ROGER: Stop right there. I'm not asking you to think. I'm asking you to embrace. I have another question for you—and like I said, I don't want you to think about it—just answer it. What don't you like about yourself?

NEAL: Do you mean, like, physically—or mentally—or—

ROGER: Whatever. Just answer the question. If there was something you could change about yourself, what would it be?

NEAL: This is embarrassing...

ROGER: Say it.

NEAL: My thighs. I don't like my thighs.

ROGER: What about them?

NEAL: They're too meaty.

ROGER: Show me.

NEAL: You want me to show you my thighs?

ROGER: It doesn't require this much conversation. Just do it. Show them to me.

Neal drops his pants.

Okay.

NEAL: You see what I mean?

ROGER: Sure, they're flabby, I can see that. What else don't you like about yourself?

(*off Neal's hesitation*)

Jesus fucking Christ, Neal, it's not that difficult. You're an insecure man. I can see it in your face. You know your faults. Spell them out for me. What else don't you like—

NEAL: My abs.

ROGER: Yeah?

NEAL: Yeah. I wish my abs were more defined.

ROGER: Are there any other things you dislike about your body?

NEAL: Those are the main things.

ROGER: I see what you're saying, Neal. But these flaws are only flaws if you're not a fucking butterfly. Get it? If you're a butterfly, these flaws make you different, unique. You're beautiful, Neal. I say that in the least gay way possible. Your thighs are awesome. Own your thighs. Your abs rock. Motherfucking own them. Embrace your body. Be fucking beautiful.

NEAL: I just...

ROGER: What? Say it. Don't hold back.

NEAL: I feel like I'd be able to be more of a butterfly if my life wasn't such a mess.

ROGER: What's a mess about it? Be specific.

NEAL: It's my wife, she—

ROGER: What's her name?

NEAL: Mandy.

ROGER: What's she look like? Paint me a picture.

NEAL: She's 5'8, medium build, light brown hair.

ROGER: Long or short?

NEAL: Shoulder length.

ROGER: Her tits?

NEAL: B cup.

ROGER: Got it. Continue.

NEAL: Anyway, Mandy, my wife, I think she's gonna cheat on me. I think she's thinking about it.

ROGER: She's into some other guy?

NEAL: It's this guy at our gym. He's always hitting on her. I can tell she likes it.

ROGER: Describe him to me.

NEAL: He's tall, really fit, cocky, bald, black, great smile. He's one of the trainers—

ROGER: And this fucking douchebag's trying to get all up in your wife's pussy.

NEAL: I wouldn't put it that way, but—

ROGER: Maybe you wouldn't, but your life's a mess, so I'll do the talking and you do the listening. You're saying this buff-ass dude, he's tall and good looking and he's covered in muscles— and he wants to fuck your wife so hard she doesn't even remember her name—

NEAL: Could you please not talk about her like that—

ROGER: Do you hear how weak you sound right now?

NEAL: I guess, but—this is making me feel very uncomfortable, Roger—

ROGER: Good. Because I'm not trying to make you comfortable. I'm trying to get you to see all of the ways you aren't a man.

NEAL: I just...

ROGER: What? You just *what*?

NEAL: I just feel so...

ROGER: You feel *so...so...so...*WHAT? Speak up. I've seen your cock—you can be better than this.

NEAL: I feel so insecure.

ROGER: God damn it, Neal. If your wife so much as looks at another dude in a flirtatious way, then it's over, you're done, you end it. You *drop* her. *You* control the situation.

NEAL: But I don't want to lose her—I love her too much—

ROGER: Listen, about a year ago, I was at this party with *my* wife, and there was this guy there who was trying to get with her. Shamelessly flirting, right in front of me. Know what I did?

NEAL: What did you do?

ROGER: I took care of it. I pushed him against the wall. I strangled him. Just enough to let him know who was in control. He apologized to my wife and then he left both of us alone.

NEAL: You strangled him and then *he* was the one who apologized?

ROGER: You act surprised. But the truth is, he saw my power. Do you see my power?

NEAL: I guess so, yeah—

ROGER: You "guess" so? Stop guessing and open your eyes. I like you, Neal. I'm gonna take you under my wing. Teach you how to be the butterfly you already are. Do you want that?

NEAL: Yes.

ROGER: Good. What else do you want? Don't think, just speak.

NEAL: I want to get out of phone sales. I want to move up into corporate. I'm better than this.
ROGER: Are you?
NEAL: I know I am.
ROGER: That's better. I can make a few phone calls. Put in a good recommendation.
NEAL: Really?
ROGER: Of course. Now take a leak so we can get back to work.
NEAL: It's okay—I think the pee went away, actually.
ROGER: A man who is a butterfly is not afraid to urinate. He just urinates. Do it.

Neal pees.

A moan of relief.

Good boy. Now I need you to do something for me. Listen carefully. Are you listening?
NEAL: I'm listening.
ROGER: I need your help with Tracy. She's a fucking cunt and we have to take care of her.

Lights shift.

SCENE SIX

Conference Room.

Tracy and Neal are at a long conference table. Neal sits with his laptop, preparing a presentation. Tracy fumes.

TRACY: It is utterly fucking ridiculous for him to make us wait like this.

NEAL: Sorry.

TRACY: Why?

NEAL: What do you mean?

TRACY: I mean, why are you apologizing? It's not your fault Roger's late.

NEAL: I know. I don't know why I said I was sorry. It just came out of my mouth. It seemed appropriate. You're angry and I don't deal well with tension. When my wife gets this way, I find she always calms down if I apologize, even if I didn't do anything.

TRACY: "This way?"

NEAL: You know...

TRACY: The reason I'm *tense* is because I want to know where the fuck Roger is. Do you know where the fuck Roger is?

NEAL: When I walked past his office, he said he'd be right in.

TRACY: And when was that?

NEAL: Uh...thirty-seven minutes ago?

TRACY: Exactly. We've been sitting here for thirty-seven fucking minutes. You're telling me you're not mad he's late?

NEAL: I'm sure he'll be here any second—

TRACY: Do you get paid to sit there and jerk off?

NEAL: What?

TRACY: It's a simple question.

NEAL: Of course I don't.

TRACY: Are you sure? Because the fact that you don't think it's total and utter bullshit that he's made us sit here and wait for—what was it—

NEAL: Thirty-seven minutes.

TRACY: The fact that each one of those thirty-seven minutes doesn't feel like a new, individual insult to you makes me wonder if you're getting paid to sit there and jerk off. It's the only way I can explain your complacency. But my skill-set can be used in more productive ways. So I'm going to leave.

NEAL: He'll be here any minute, I'm sure—

TRACY: I have to get back to my desk, I have a consultation with Colleen Langley at three o'clock. If Roger decides to show up, tell him I'm doing actual work.

She starts to roll out.

NEAL: No, wait—

He stands up and blocks her.

TRACY: What are you doing, Neal?

NEAL: Like I said before, we should wait for Roger.

TRACY: Get out of my way.

NEAL: I can't let you leave.

TRACY: You can't *let* me leave?

NEAL: I'm sorry.

TRACY: Now *that* apology was conflicted.

NEAL: No it wasn't.

TRACY: It had weight, and a little bit of pathos.

NEAL: No it didn't.

TRACY: That apology was real.

NEAL: So?

TRACY: Why are you sorry, Neal?

NEAL: Don't get into my head, okay? Just sit there and wait for Roger to get here.

TRACY: You're not gonna tell me what's going on?

NEAL: Nothing's going on.

TRACY: You realize you're holding me hostage.

NEAL: I'm not making you stay here.

TRACY: Move out of my way.

NEAL: Then get up and walk around me if you really want to leave.

TRACY: You know I can't do that.

NEAL: That's not what I heard.

TRACY: Oh really?

NEAL: Fuck. I shouldn't have said that.

TRACY: So Roger talked to you?

NEAL: No.

TRACY: What else did he tell you?

NEAL: He didn't tell me anything because we didn't talk.

TRACY: What's Roger doing right now? Why is he making you keep me in here?

NEAL: I don't know what you're talking about.

Beat.

TRACY: Do you love your son?

NEAL: Of course I do. What's that have to do with anything?

TRACY: His name's Cameron, right?

NEAL: Yeah, but I still don't—

TRACY: Every time I move past your desk, I see that one picture of you and your wife and your adorable son Cameron on the beach—

NEAL: We were in Costa Rica.

TRACY: And your wife's expression always strikes me because she looks pained, she looks...uncomfortable. I used to ask myself: why is that? I mean, she's on the beach with her husband, and her little boy. And this woman, your wife—

NEAL: Mandy.

TRACY: Mandy. She has it all.

NEAL: What does that have to do with—

TRACY: I hear you talking to *Mandy* on the phone, Neal. On your lunch breaks. I hear how you treat her, and I've gotta say: you

48

sound like a good husband. You do. You sound attentive, you sound like you care.

NEAL: Thank you.

TRACY: And I don't think she's cheating on you.

NEAL: Why would you say that?

TRACY: Because you call her *every day*—

NEAL: It's our routine—

TRACY: It's smothering, you *smother* her. It's because you're insecure.

NEAL (*rattled*): I'm not.

TRACY: But she loves you. She wouldn't do that to you.

NEAL: What are you doing? Why are you—

TRACY: The real question is: why does this woman with the attentive, caring husband and the too-adorable-for-words baby—why does she look so damned uncomfortable in that photo?

Beat. He really thinks about it.

NEAL: I don't know.

TRACY: It's because of the bathing suit, Neal. She doesn't like being photographed in her bathing suit. If she knew that photo was on your desk, she would be so fucking mortified.

NEAL: Why do you care about my wife?

TRACY: I'm just pointing out that she's a woman who worries. And she's going to be so upset when I tell her about the blowjob I gave you last Friday night.

NEAL: But you didn't—that's a lie—and she wouldn't—she won't believe you.

TRACY: But she will, Neal. She'll believe the girl in the chair. And what's worse is: she'll think it means something. If I was some bimbo you met at a bar, I'd be harmless. But I'm your wheelchair-bound co-worker. You don't "get with" your wheelchair-bound co-worker unless it actually means something. Unless you have feelings.

NEAL: She trusts me.

TRACY: Maybe. But you were here awfully late last Friday. It'll make your wife wonder. It'll root its way into her brain and stick there. She won't be able to shake it. Of course, I don't have to call her. Whatever. I don't care. I'm just thinking of sweet little Cameron.

Beat. A sudden choice.

NEAL: Roger wanted me to distract you. The Power Point presentation I'm supposedly waiting to present—it's all a ruse. Roger's at your computer.

TRACY: What's he looking for?

NEAL: He's going through your files. Looking for something he can use against you. Since you're blackmailing him, he wants to, like, double-blackmail you—

TRACY: I'm not blackmailing him.

NEAL: You obviously are, Tracy. I mean, you just blackmailed *me* to get me to admit that Roger's trying to blackmail you, so don't expect me to believe you're not the type of person who blackmails people, okay?

TRACY: Don't raise your voice. Sit down.

NEAL: I still can't let you leave.

TRACY: I'm not going to leave anymore. I want Roger to think he's in control. So have a seat and don't tell him we had this conversation.

NEAL: And you expect me to do what you say because of the blowjob threat?

TRACY: Yes.

NEAL: Okay.

Neal sits. Nervously picks at his cuticles.

TRACY: And try to act normal. You're acting weird.

NEAL: I'm not doing anything.

TRACY: You're picking your cuticles.

He stops. They wait in silence for a beat.

NEAL: He might be awhile.

TRACY: I have all day.

NEAL: Fine. Me too, then.

TRACY: Good.

Another beat.

NEAL: So we're just gonna sit here?

TRACY: As if I had a choice in the matter.

NEAL: Right.

> *Another awkward few beats. Neal sits nervously. Tracy sucks her thumb provocatively at Neal, taunting him, moaning with pleasure.*

TRACY: *Oh, Neal. Oh, God, oh.*

> *Roger enters. Tracy sits upright, wiping her thumb on her leg.*

ROGER: I'm so sorry about that. I got stuck on a call with Steven in the New York office.

TRACY: It's fine. We barely noticed.

NEAL: Yeah, we were just sitting here. I answered some e-mails. I think that's what Tracy was doing too, right?

TRACY: I was playing Smart Happy Apple on my phone. Heard of it?

ROGER: No.

TRACY: It's this game where you pretend to be a clever apple. All the rage these days.

ROGER: Again, sorry to keep you waiting.

TRACY: And again, it's fine. Like I said, we barely noticed.

ROGER: We should get started with the meeting.

TRACY: Great.

ROGER: Neal, I believe you have some graphs to show us.

NEAL: She knows, Roger.

| TRACY: Jesus. | ROGER: Motherfucker. |

NEAL (*like a freight train*): Fuck. Fuck! I shouldn't have said that. Sorry, Tracy, I was trying to keep it in, but I'm a terrible liar. Roger, I'm apologizing to Tracy because the truth is I told her everything and then she blackmailed me and now I'm not supposed to tell you that she knows everything, but of course I wasn't supposed to tell her anything in the first place, so I owe you an apology for that, and you should know that I really *am* sorry, I really, truly am, because I stabbed you in the back, and then I stabbed her in the back, and now I can't keep track of who I'm supposed to be aligned with and who I'm supposed to be lying to and this is really—this is really—this is really a lot of pressure that both of you are putting on me and I can't handle it, okay? I can't—fucking—handle it. And I don't want to be a butterfly and I don't want to lose my wife. I want you to leave me alone and let me do my job! But you come at me with your needs and your lies and your manipulations and I'm sorry, okay? This is a toxic environment, it's TOXIC, and I can't deal anymore. I just want everyone to be happy! But if you need to fuck each other over, do it directly, okay, and take me out of the middle. I'm not good in the middle! It feels like I'm getting fucked from both sides and it's making me dizzy, okay? Good, good, okay, good. Now everything is out there, it's all out in the open, you both know that both of you know everything, and I'm sorry I'm not better at being bad, and fuck both of you—fuck both of you in the ass.

ROGER: You are a fucking idiot.

NEAL: Can I leave now?

ROGER: No. Sit there. Think about what an idiot you are.

Neal sits on the ground.

In the chair, asshole.

Neal goes to the chair.

TRACY: Did you find anything on my computer?

ROGER: You know I didn't.

TRACY: Then have you figured out a way to help me yet?

ROGER: I talked to our insurance guy.

TRACY: And?

ROGER: I told him the truth. What you want. What you want to do to yourself.

TRACY: That won't work.

ROGER: It's the tactic I took.

TRACY: No. You said you'd make it look like something else, you said you'd make it look good.

Go back to him—

ROGER: He said no, Tracy.

TRACY: He can't say no.

ROGER: They won't cover it. No one will cover this surgery for you.

TRACY (*genuinely hurt*): So that's it? You made a phone call and you're done?

ROGER: Yes.

TRACY (*letting her guard down*): No.

No, no, no, that's not how this is supposed to go. You're supposed to help me, Roger.

She is like a little lost girl. Desperate. Vulnerable. Scared.

ROGER: Tracy.

TRACY: Please? Just help me—please—you can do that—use your power, use your influence—please, can't you—

ROGER: Tracy.

TRACY: I need somebody to help me. Why can't you be that person? Why won't you help me? My limbs are unviable. I need to be fixed. Why can't anyone understand that?

ROGER: Have you ever heard of men who breastfeed?

Tracy?

Tracy, look at me.

She does.

There are men out there who want to experience the act of breastfeeding so badly they *will* it to happen.

I mean, obviously it's possible, we all have mammary glands—but it's not like it's easy for a man to make milk.

You have to really work the nipple—

Squeezing it, rubbing it, caressing it.

What you're doing is you're tricking your body,

you're trying to get your body to think that man-milk is natural, but your body knows this is a fucking trick.

Your body's like: "Dude, you're a man, stop trying to make me make milk."

But these men—

these breastfeeding wannabes,

they keep going, they keep trying, they keep rubbing their nipples raw.

They just won't give up—that's how much they want the milk.

And it's like—finally the body gives up and says: "Fine. You want milk? Here's some fucking milk."

And now you've got this, this, this, this *man*—

this man who's breastfeeding his child.

And I know what you're thinking—you're thinking it's some sort of miracle.

You're thinking it's beautiful.

But it's not.

It's fucking disgusting, is what it is.

Those guys who want to breastfeed their children are aberrations of nature.

They're freaks.

And you are too, Tracy.

You're a breastfeeding man.

An aberration of nature.

You need help.

I'm sorry to be blunt—I actually am sorry—but I think it's the only way you can hear it.

You want this surgery?

Because your legs don't work in your head?

Don't you hear how perverse that is?

TRACY (*fuck you*): I don't have to listen to this.

>   *She starts to wheel out. Roger blocks her.*

Get the fuck out of my way, Roger. I'm serious.

ROGER: So you can call the corporate office? Not a chance.

>   *Roger grabs Tracy.*

I'm gonna make you walk.

>   *Tracy struggles, thrashing against Roger.*

TRACY: Fuck you!

ROGER: Walk out. Neal, come on—help me.

TRACY: Don't you dare touch me, Neal.

>*Neal grabs her arms from behind, while Roger grabs her legs. They lift her out of the chair.*

Let go of me!

>*She heaves her upper body towards Neal, biting his bicep like an animal. Neal screams.*

NEAL: She bit me! She fucking bit me!

>*Neal grunts with pain, but still holds on to her.*

ROGER: Walk. Walk!

TRACY: Stop! Stop!

>*Tracy screams.*

ROGER: Goddamnit!

She jerks her body again, causing Neal to lose his grip. Tracy's upper body falls to the ground, her head hitting the floor with a hard thwack.

NEAL: Oh my God.

Roger still has her legs in his arms, as Tracy's body goes limp.

ROGER: Holy shit.

Roger finally drops Tracy's legs to the floor.

NEAL: Oh my God. This isn't good.
ROGER: You think?
NEAL: Tracy? Tracy, are you okay?
ROGER: She definitely isn't okay.
NEAL: This isn't fucking good. This is really *not* fucking good. Fuck. Shit!
ROGER: Do something.
NEAL: What am I supposed to do?
ROGER: Stop freaking out.
NEAL: I can't do that, Roger. I can't stop, I can't breathe. Oh God, if she's dead—

ROGER: You know, she was blackmailing me—and she was blackmailing you, too, right?

NEAL: Yeah. She was gonna tell Mandy that she gave me a blowjob.

ROGER: That would have been horrible for your marriage. So it's not like—I mean, if Tracy dead, it's—it's not the *worst* thing that ever happened. And now we—

NEAL: Jesus, Roger.

WOMAN'S VOICE (*OFF STAGE*): Excuse me?

NEAL: Did you hear that? I heard a woman. A woman's voice.

WOMAN'S VOICE (*OFF STAGE*): Is there anyone here?

ROGER: Hide the body. *Hide the fucking body.*

> *Neal pushes Tracy's body under the table, or behind the cupboard, or some other fucking place. But it doesn't fit. The legs stick out. Fuck, shit, fuck me up the ass.*

I still see her.

NEAL: She doesn't fit!

ROGER: Shove her in!

> *Neal contorts the legs to get them out of view.*

NEAL (*suddenly noticing*): What about her chair—

ROGER: Sit in it.

NEAL: What?

ROGER: Fucking sit in it!

> *Neal hesitates, so Roger pushes him into the chair. Just as: COLLEEN enters.*

COLLEEN: I'm looking for Tracy.

ROGER: You're looking for Tracy?

COLLEEN: Do I need to say it twice?

ROGER: How can I help you?

COLLEEN: So three times, then?

ROGER: Do you want to see our catalogue?

COLLEEN: That's how we're doing this?

NEAL (*sudden realization*): Oh my God—

COLLEEN: I have an appointment with *Tracy*.

NEAL (*sotto, to Roger*): —it's Tracy's three o'clock. Colleen Langley.

(*overcompensating*)

Hi, hello, how are you, Colleen?

COLLEEN: I'm tired, actually. I need to get these shoes off.

> *She muscles past them, takes a seat.*

ROGER: Did the receptionist say to wait in Conference Room A or Conference Room B?
COLLEEN: She pointed to this conference room.
NEAL: This is Conference Room A.

> *Colleen removes one of her shoes.*

COLLEEN: I've got this nerve problem.
ROGER: She probably meant Conference Room B—
COLLEEN: It only bothers me when I wear these shoes. They pinch my feet.

> *She shows no intention of getting out of the chair.*

NEAL: But it's fine. We weren't even—I mean, nothing to see here, we're done with—our meeting, that we were just having—just finishing up anyway, there is absolutely nothing important going on in this room at all, so—
ROGER: We're not completely done, actually—the other conference room would be better.
COLLEEN: Then you can take your business there 'cause I'm not moving.

> *Colleen removes her other shoe. Lets out a groan as she rubs her foot.*

Roger looks at Neal, like: what the fuck. Neal looks at Roger, like: I was acting natural.

Is Tracy on her way?
NEAL: Doubtful.
ROGER: Why don't we...

Beat. Then Roger launches in...

You're here for a body consultation, I assume?
COLLEEN: Why would you assume that?
ROGER: You have a three o'clock appointment.
COLLEEN: I could be here to talk to Tracy about anything.
ROGER: Yes, but—
COLLEEN: Why do you assume it's about my body?
ROGER: —we sell weight loss systems.
COLLEEN: I'm sorry.
ROGER: Don't be.
COLLEEN: I'm nervous.
ROGER: Understandable.
COLLEEN: My husband doesn't like the way I look.
ROGER: I see.
COLLEEN: I wouldn't be here if it weren't for him.
ROGER: No?
COLLEEN: No.

ROGER: Do you...

COLLEEN: Like the way I look?

ROGER: Yes.

COLLEEN: I do.

ROGER: Okay.

COLLEEN: I did.

ROGER: There it is.

COLLEEN: I think I'm very attractive.

ROGER: Of course.

COLLEEN: But then people like you think I need body consultations—

ROGER: It's my job.

COLLEEN: —and the wires in my head get all screwy.

ROGER: We can help you.

COLLEEN: Can you?

ROGER: Talk to me.

COLLEEN: Okay.

ROGER: What do you want to change about yourself?

COLLEEN: I'd rather talk to Tracy.

ROGER: I'm her boss.

COLLEEN: I get that.

ROGER: Good.

COLLEEN: But these are sensitive issues.

ROGER: Anything she could tell you—

COLLEEN: I'd rather talk to a woman.

ROGER: —she learned from me.

COLLEEN: I'd feel more comfortable.

ROGER: Okay.

COLLEEN: Really?

ROGER: Fine, then.

COLLEEN: Thank you.

ROGER: Of course. Neal?

NEAL: I'll go find her.

Neal rolls out of the room.

COLLEEN: I sense some tension. Between you and him.

ROGER: Do you?

COLLEEN: I have a very good intuition about things like this.

ROGER: Well, you're wrong.

COLLEEN: Know what? You don't need to wait with me. I can wait for Tracy.

ROGER: She isn't coming.

COLLEEN: But you just sent that man—

ROGER: He isn't coming back either.

COLLEEN: He went looking for Tracy. You said—

ROGER: I know what I said and I know what he did. If you want a consultation, you can talk to me.

COLLEEN: I don't feel comfortable.

ROGER: Because I'm a man.

COLLEEN: Yes. Like I said—

ROGER: My job is to help you—people like you—and I'm very good at it. This isn't about your husband, is it? He didn't send you here. You're the one who isn't happy with your body. Am I correct?

Beat.

COLLEEN: Yes.
ROGER: See, I have intuition too. And that tension you were sensing—you were right about that. But look:

He shakes out his body.

I'm shaking it out. Shake it out with me.
COLLEEN: You want me to shake?
ROGER: Yes. Because you have tension too. I can see it, it's rippling off of your body. We all have tension. So shake it out with me. Come on, Colleen. Shake.

She tentatively shakes her body along with him. Jumping up and down.

You can do better than that, Colleen—really commit to it.
COLLEEN: I'm shaking. I'm shaking it out.
ROGER: Now vocalize. Get the tension out.

He grunts as he shakes.

HUH. HUH. HUH.

COLLEEN (*grunting along with him*): HUH. HUH. HUH. HUH.

ROGER: HUH. HUH.

COLLEEN: HUH. HUH. HUH. HUH.

ROGER: Good. That's good.

COLLEEN: HUH. HUH. HUH.

ROGER: Good.

COLLEEN: HUH. HUH.

ROGER: Now scream.

COLLEEN: Scream?

ROGER: Don't stop shaking! Shake!

COLLEEN: I'm shaking!

ROGER: And scream!

She lets out a scream.

Scream louder, Colleen. Let it out.

She screams louder.

Good, good!

One more scream.

Okay, you can stop now.

> *She doesn't stop. A few more screams burst out, as—*

Okay. Okay. Okay!

> *When she stops—*

Do you feel...

COLLEEN: I feel better.

ROGER: Good. I knew you would. Now can we do this?

COLLEEN: I guess.

ROGER: *Don't guess.* Take ownership of your decisions, Colleen. Do you think you're beautiful?

COLLEEN (*without hesitation*): No.

> *Roger is in full-on consultation mode now. Focusing all his attention on her. His questions are like bullets.*

ROGER: Our outsides reflect our insides, Colleen. If we only talk about your outsides, we aren't addressing the real issue. Can you show me what's inside?

COLLEEN: Yes.

ROGER: Can you open up?

COLLEEN: Yes.

ROGER: Can you be raw?

COLLEEN: I can.

ROGER: Then why are you here?

COLLEEN: I don't love my husband.

ROGER: There we go.

COLLEEN: I didn't know that was coming.

ROGER: Don't hold back now.

COLLEEN: Oh God, I never loved my husband.

ROGER: Keep going, Colleen.

COLLEEN: I was in love with Jimmy Powell. I was 15, he was 17. An older man.

ROGER: You liked that?

COLLEEN: I was shy. I sang in the choir, but never a solo. I had to blend in with the group.

ROGER: But Jimmy was different, wasn't he?

COLLEEN: He was confident, charming, loud. Everything I wasn't.

ROGER: Describe him. What did he look like?

COLLEEN: He was long and lanky. Broad shoulders. His arms were so long it felt like he could hug the whole world. He had a crooked nose from when he broke it falling out of a tree when he was little. Short, cropped hair. His smile made me weak.

ROGER: How'd you meet him?

COLLEEN: I watched him play basketball. On game days he'd wear his uniform to class. I can still see him swaggering down the halls. His shorts clinging to his thighs. The first time we spoke, there was an immediate attraction, a rush of adrenaline. Like how it feels when you walk out of a store with something you didn't pay for and you know you got away with it, that feverish happy thump in your chest.

ROGER: Don't just give me feelings, Colleen. Give me details. Were you physical?

COLLEEN: Not at first. But when we finally got together, it was animalistic. Pure and impure at the same time. He was all I could think about.

ROGER: He was your first?

COLLEEN: Well, technically I was saving myself for marriage...

ROGER: But?

COLLEEN: But I figured fingering was fine.

ROGER: Oh, did you now?

COLLEEN: He fingered me all the time. He fingered me in his car. He fingered me in the cafeteria. He fingered me in study hall. When he was down there it was like he opened a door that kept

opening

and opening

and opening

like an Escher drawing.

It was wonderful.

ROGER: Did you reciprocate?

COLLEEN: Of course I did. I was a good little cocksucker. Jimmy liked when I said filthy things like that. The dirtier my thoughts, the harder his cock, the faster his fingers. Not fast at first, but fast when it mattered. His fingers were always discovering me like it was the first time. He was an Egyptian archaeologist and my pussy was his pyramid. He was a deep sea diver and my pussy was his pearl. He was Alexander Fleming and my pussy was / penicillin.

ROGER: —penicillin.

COLLEEN: That's right. *High school was great.* But then Jimmy graduated. He went off to college. Far away. We tried the long distance thing, but that all got fucked up when I got the phone call from Lolita Wang. She was a friend of mine, but she was in Jimmy's class. They went to the same college.

ROGER: Describe her. Give me an image.

COLLEEN: She was short. Long black hair. Double D's.

ROGER: Continue.

COLLEEN: Lolita saw some girl flirting with Jimmy and she heard they fucked in the showers. She said she was watching out for me, she said I had to know. I was devastated. I cried for five days. I barely stopped to sleep. I listened to "Rainy Days and Mondays" by The Carpenters over and over again. The way Karen sang about having the blues made me feel less alone.

She sings, mournfully.

Tracy's legs—stiff, rigid, dead—suddenly fall out of whatever tiny space Neal shoved them into.

Roger notices the legs. Colleen doesn't.

> *Roger takes a few steps towards Tracy's legs. Colleen stops singing, looks at him.*

ROGER: That's good. Put yourself back in the moment like that. Close your eyes. Feel it.

COLLEEN (*closing her eyes*): I kept obsessing over who this other girl might be. What she might look like. But when I was singing along with Karen Carpenter, I could let that other girl go.

> *Roger walks to the legs, keeping an eye on Colleen as he tries to contort the legs back into their hiding place.*

I finally got angry. If he can go fuck some random girl, what was I saving myself for? So one day, after school, I was working on my Moby Dick report with this random guy from my advanced English class and I reached over and put my hand on his crotch and before I knew it we were fucking. Suddenly this boy took Karen Carpenter's place. Instead of crying and singing, I was having Moby Dick study sessions. Every time, I closed my eyes and wished he was Jimmy. Because Jimmy still had my heart. You know? Wanna know what's funny?

> *Just as Roger gets the legs out of view, Colleen opens her eyes. Looks at him for approval.*

ROGER: Yeah. What's funny?

COLLEEN: I still close my eyes and wish he's Jimmy. Because I married that illiterate fucking Moby-Dick-reading, puny-pricked shit-basket ass-for-brains fuckwit. His name's Todd. Todd Cohen. We even have a kid.

ROGER: And you stayed with him?

COLLEEN: What else could I do? Jimmy was my destiny, but he didn't want me anymore. So I settled. For someone else's dreams. It was like I didn't live in my body anymore. Like I was just a house guest, married to someone else's husband, with someone else's kid, going to someone else's remedial job every day, walking around in someone else's body. And since that body wasn't mine, I didn't take care of it. I got lazy, I ate whatever I wanted, I didn't exercise, I got too much sun. I didn't even floss. Which, if you know me, you'd realize was a really big deal because my father was a dentist and I was an avid flosser as a child. But if I couldn't have Jimmy, then I didn't give one single fuck about plaque, you know?

ROGER: Uh-huh.

COLLEEN: Then a lot of time passed. Todd and I found a rhythm with each other. He got used to my quiet hatred. We faked it for Madison until she went off to school. And through all of that, I've always wondered what happened to Jimmy. But I wouldn't let myself look him up until my daughter was out of the house.

ROGER: I get the impression she's gone now.

COLLEEN: She moved out last week.

ROGER: And, so...?

COLLEEN: So I looked him up online, a few nights ago. He still lives nearby. He has two kids—teenagers. But he's divorced. And I've decided it's time. I'm going to leave my husband and get Jimmy back. That's why I came to Tender Form Weight Loss Systems. I want to look good for Jimmy. This house is mine and I'm here to reclaim it.

> *She sings a few more lyrics from "Rainy Days and Mondays." Then—*

You know?

ROGER: ...okay.

COLLEEN: Was that raw enough for you?

ROGER: It was, Colleen.

COLLEEN: Good.

ROGER: I appreciate your frankness.

COLLEEN: Thank you.

ROGER: But tell me—you say you want to reclaim your body.

COLLEEN: Yes.

ROGER: How do you plan to do that?

COLLEEN: I don't know, I'm not sure—that's why I'm here.

ROGER: Did you hear that?

COLLEEN: Hear what?

ROGER: How you said absolutely nothing in two different ways?

COLLEEN: No.

ROGER: "I don't know." "I'm not sure." Both statements say nothing. They're wishy washy. Our words have power, Colleen. What you present to the world, it's—and I'm sorry to say this, but it's true—the way you present yourself to the world right now is pathetic.

COLLEEN: I just poured out my soul to you and you're calling me pathetic?

ROGER: I'm not sure the woman sitting in front of me has the strength to follow through with the kind of change that's necessary here.

COLLEEN: I can't believe this is my consultation.

ROGER: Would you rather I sugarcoat things?

COLLEEN: This just isn't what I was expecting to hear. I wasn't expecting anyone to call me pathetic.

ROGER: I won't apologize for telling you the truth, Colleen. You're pathetic. Listening to you just now? All of the lies you've had to tell yourself to get through each day. It's pathetic. You need to accept that fact before you can change. You've treated your body like trash. And if you want your body to be a home—to use your metaphor—then you're going to need to demolish that home and rebuild from the ground up. Which means Tender Form Weight Loss sessions for a minimum of six months, with at least one treatment per week. You're going to need to read our entire book series, and you're going to need to follow along with the supplementary audio books. Now, I'll take you through our catalog—

Neal rolls into the room, stopping in the doorway.

NEAL: Roger?

ROGER: I'm busy right now, Neal.

NEAL: I know, but Roger?

ROGER: *Neal.*

NEAL: There's a woman in the lobby asking to see Tracy. She says her name's Colleen Langley.

ROGER: But this is Colleen Langley.

COLLEEN: Actually, I'm not Colleen Langley. I met Colleen Langley in the lobby and I asked her to give us a few minutes. I'm from corporate. My name's Wanda Cohen. We've actually met several times, Roger. I've been with the company for seven years. Tracy filed a sexual harassment complaint against you and this was my way of checking to see how you run things down here. It's basically a performance review. Surprise! You look displeased. I'm sorry about that, but I suppose it's for the best because you're in deep fucking shit. Shall we get on with the review?

ROGER: Neal, could you do the real Colleen's consultation in Conference Room B?

NEAL: I would like nothing better than to leave this room and do that.

Neal rolls out. An awkward beat as Roger takes in the woman before him, who we will now refer to as Wanda.

ROGER: Am I being fired?

WANDA: Am I making you nervous? Because you seem nervous, Roger.

ROGER: I am. A little bit, actually.

WANDA: Don't be nervous.

ROGER: It's just, I really do need this job.

WANDA: I don't like men like you, Roger.

ROGER: What am I like?

WANDA: Do you hear how I keep saying your name, Roger? You do that. When you're talking to someone you're trying to control. It's one of the ways you like to assert your dominance. You like dominating conversations, don't you, Roger?

ROGER: Yes.

WANDA: Well, that's just one of the things I don't like about you. Ironically, I understand the impulse. Dominating you right now feels good.

ROGER: What did Tracy say?

WANDA: When?

ROGER: In her complaint against me? You said she filed—

WANDA: Yes, that's right.

ROGER: And?

WANDA: It said you threatened to fire her and that you'd said some inappropriate things.

ROGER: That's all?

WANDA: Yes. But then last night we spoke on the phone. That's when she told me the two of you copulated in your office. I'm sorry, let me rephrase that: she said you threatened to fire her unless she fucked you.

ROGER: That's what she told you? Those were her exact words?

WANDA: I'd have to consult my report for the exact words. But that's the gist.

ROGER: That's not how it went down at all.

WANDA: Then, please, enlighten me.

ROGER: First of all, I need to apologize for letting things get this far. It's just a crazy story and I got in over my head and I've been trying to figure out how to handle the situation without involving corporate, but, well, clearly things have escalated. I should have been the one to call you—before Tracy gave you her skewed version of events, I mean. The truth is...

WANDA: Yes?

ROGER: This is hard to talk about...

WANDA: Just say it.

ROGER (*getting "emotional"*): Tracy raped me.

WANDA: She raped you.

ROGER: Yes.

WANDA: You're saying you were raped.

ROGER: That's what I'm saying.

WANDA: And when did this...*incident*...occur?

ROGER: It was during her performance review. The review was not going well, as you can imagine. Tracy hadn't been hitting her quota, and I told her there was a strong likelihood that we'd have

to let her go. Have you seen the numbers she posted last month?
WANDA: I have.
ROGER: So I tell her we might have to let her go, and then she starts crying. So of course I get her some tissues and I move around to the front of my desk to hand them to her, and that's when she grabs me. She just grabs me. And she pushes me into the desk.

> *He's really milking it, getting more and more emotional...*

Suddenly she's got me pinned to the desk with her wheelchair. It's digging into my legs and she's pulling my pants down. Oh God, she's—she's—

> *Oh God, he's even working up a few tears. Wanda offers him a tissue from her purse.*

So, you know, that's what happened. Hashtag Me Too. She threatened me, she threatened my wife, she threatened my daughter, little Kayla. She was prepared to ruin my life if I fired her. That's what's been going on. She's been waging a psychological war against me.

> *He blows his nose.*

So if you'd put that in the official report, I'd appreciate it.
WANDA: *Wow.*

>*Beat.*

I don't believe a word that just came out of your mouth.

>*He drops the emotion, tossing the used tissue back at Wanda.*

ROGER: Yeah, well, that's my story. It's the story I'm sticking to.
WANDA: Then I'll have to file my report, and we'll see if that story gets stuck.
ROGER: Good. It was a pleasure meeting you, Wanda. Oh, sorry, I forgot, you've been with the company for seven years. You just never left an impression.
WANDA: Can I be completely honest with you, Roger?
ROGER: Go for it.
WANDA: I didn't take Tracy's complaint seriously at first. My job is to protect the company, to watch out for Tender Form Weight Loss Systems. And you're the company. More than she is. Which means my job is to make her and her problem go away. My job is to watch out for you. But then it hit me: men like you don't deserve my help.
ROGER: *Men like me?*
WANDA: That's right.

ROGER: You think you know me?

WANDA: I don't want to know you.

ROGER: Oh, so that's how it is—you have a preconceived idea of who I am, but you don't know me at all. I grew up with nothing. My parents didn't even go to college—

WANDA: Shut up, Roger.

ROGER: You don't want to hear my story?

WANDA: I don't *need* to hear your story. I don't need to know you, or where you're from, or who you go home to at night. I don't need to know any of the little things that *you think* make you special.

ROGER: Because you're closed-minded.

WANDA: Because I already know enough privileged motherfuckers like you. Do you know how many little shits like you I've had to deal with just in the seven years I've worked at this company? I've been dealing with men like you my entire life. The last thing I need to know now is your story. Spare me the fucking details.

ROGER: I bet you're a dyke.

WANDA: Clever, Roger. But you just showed me what you are. You're cancer. If cancer had two legs, and two arms, and a head, and a heart, and a shriveled little cock, it would be you.

ROGER: I remind you of your dad, don't I?

WANDA: No. He's one of the good guys.

ROGER: Then your husband—I remind you of him, the one you hate. Todd.

WANDA: Nice try.

ROGER: You can't fire me.

WANDA: I don't want to just fire you. I want to demolish you. I want to ensure you never work again.
ROGER: Good luck with that. The only problem is: it's my word against Tracy's, and I have a feeling she isn't going to be able to contradict anything I've just said.
TRACY (*groggy, from wherever she was shoved*): Hello?
ROGER: Fuck me.
WANDA: Who is that?
TRACY: Oh God. Someone help me.
ROGER: Tracy.
WANDA: Jesus, Roger.

> *Tracy crawls into view. Part of her head is covered in blood, her hair matted to her scalp in a maroon clump.*
>
> *Wanda rushes over to help her.*

TRACY: Where am I?
WANDA: Tracy, are you okay?
TRACY: Yes?
WANDA: Your legs work?
TRACY: Where am I?
WANDA: Does your head hurt?
TRACY: I think so.
WANDA: Let me look at it.

> *Wanda gently touches Tracy's head.*
> *Looks at the cut.*

TRACY: Who are you?

WANDA: I'm Wanda Cohen. We spoke last night.

TRACY: Who?

WANDA: From corporate. Human Resources. What happened? Why were you in the closet?

TRACY: I don't know.

> *Tracy's whole body language is different than before. The way she holds herself is younger, somehow.*

WANDA: I thought you couldn't walk?

ROGER: She's a liar. That's what I was trying to tell you before.

WANDA: You're telling me she invented an accident that left her paralyzed from the waist down?

TRACY: Excuse me—

ROGER: That's how she says it happened? An accident?

WANDA: That's what it says in her file. She was in a car accident in 1997.

TRACY: My head hurts.

ROGER: It's just one of her stories. One of her many stories—

TRACY: My head really hurts.

WANDA: Does it hurt to stand? Are your legs tingling?

ROGER: Her legs are fine.

> *Neal appears in the doorway, still in the wheelchair.*

NEAL: Excuse me, Roger, could I see you outside for a—

(*suddenly shocked to see*)

Tracy.

TRACY: How do you know me?

NEAL: No. Fuck this. I don't know you. I don't know any of you. I quit.

WANDA: Neal, before you quit, could you get us a hot washcloth? Tracy seems to have hit her head.

NEAL: But—

WANDA: Just do it, be useful.

NEAL: I'll be right back.

> *Neal swivels the wheelchair and exits.*

TRACY: Would someone tell me WHAT'S GOING ON. Where am I?

WANDA: You don't know where you are?

TRACY: My head hurts really—it hurts really bad and I—I—I don't know how I got here. What time is it?

ROGER: I don't believe this.

WANDA: It's three-forty-five.

TRACY: Three-forty-five? Oh shit, no way. Can I call my mom? I was supposed to be home by, like, three-thirty? Oh my God, they're gonna be so mad if I'm, if I'm late again—

ROGER: Give me a fucking break.

Neal re-enters with the washcloth.

NEAL: Here you go.

He wheels over to Tracy, hands her the washcloth.

TRACY: Thank you.

As Wanda oversees Tracy's wound care—

NEAL: I'm going.
ROGER: No you're not.
NEAL: I quit.
ROGER: No you didn't.
NEAL: Fuck you.
ROGER: Just sit there.

Neal stays right where he is.

TRACY: Will one of you please tell me where I am?

WANDA: You're at work, Tracy.

TRACY: What do you mean?

WANDA: You're at Tender Form Weight Loss Systems.

TRACY: I don't know what that is.

WANDA: It's your job.

TRACY: My mom won't let me get a job until next year.

WANDA: And what year would that be?

TRACY: 1990.

WANDA: So right now, it's...

TRACY: 1989.

> *By now it should really begin to click: Tracy's attitude, her body language— she's acting like a teenager.*

NEAL: Is this for real?

ROGER (*laughing*): Oh my God. This is good.

WANDA: *Roger.*

ROGER: You don't actually believe any of this bullshit, do you?

WANDA: She hit her head. We need to get her to a hospital—

ROGER: She's playing you.

WANDA: You think she's faking this too? That's your answer for everything.

ROGER: She is. Watch this. Hey Tracy, what month do you think it is?

TRACY: What do you mean?

ROGER: It's not a hard question, damn it. What fucking month do you think it is? Tell me, Tracy.
TRACY: It's April 11, 1989.
ROGER: Google it, Neal. April 11, 1989.

Neal types the date into his phone.

What day of the week is it?
WANDA: I think maybe Tracy should lie down—
TRACY: Tuesday.
NEAL: She's right. Tuesday.
ROGER: Good guess.
WANDA: Tracy doesn't need to prove she has a head injury, Roger. Lay off.
ROGER: I'm just getting started.
TRACY: You're scaring me. Will someone get my mom?
ROGER: I have several more questions.
WANDA: Stuff it, Roger.
TRACY: I need some water.
NEAL: I'll go.

Neal gets up from the wheelchair, gets the fuck out of there.

TRACY: And some aspirin, too, actually? My head is, like, throbbing.

Wanda pulls Roger aside.

ROGER: You don't actually believe her—
WANDA: When this leads to a lawsuit, it'll be better for the company if the man who contorted Tracy's concussed body like a pretzel, then tried to hide it, isn't working here anymore. Now go get her some aspirin.
ROGER: I'm not getting her a fucking thing.
WANDA: You're exhausting.

She exits.

ROGER: Listen, Tracy—

He walks towards her, but Tracy backs away from him.

TRACY: Who are you?
ROGER: Just listen to me. You're lying right now, this act of yours—

He keeps moving towards her, like an animal stalking their prey—

TRACY: Why would you say that?

—as Tracy moves to the other side of the conference table, trying to get away from him. Her fear building.

ROGER: Because I know you're fucking lying and I want you to understand that I am going to break you. I am going to break you into pieces. Got it? I am going to rend every single part of your body until all of you is useless.
TRACY: Why are you being so mean to me?
ROGER: Tracy—
TRACY: WHY ARE YOU BEING SO MEAN TO ME?

This is a messy moment.

Tracy lets loose. Tears stream down her face.

She's ugly, desperate, barely able to keep her shit together. There should be something almost scary about how raw and open she is.

All I ever try to do is be nice. I try to be good.
My mom taught me how to be kind, how to be honest, how to be true. She always says: "You have to be one of the nice ones." So I try. I try to be a good student, I try to make all the right choices,

no matter how hard it is. I'm always careful to treat others how I want them to treat me.

But lately, it's like...last year, things started to get so confusing. It all started with Elizabeth Hernandez making fun of my clothes. Because she dresses so provocatively, and I...don't.

I tried to hold my head up high.

Then someone started that rumor about me and Justin Dellarosa. Saying we did things under the bleachers. Things I've never even heard of. I tried to smile at them. To be nice, to be honest, to be good. And at first I thought it was working, but then I heard Kelly Marsh talking in the bathroom about how much she hates my smile and she can't decide if I smile so much because I'm stupid or if I smile so much because I'm a bitch. So I stopped trying to make nice with the girls because no matter how hard I tried, it never seemed to work. Which just left the boys, who were...

worse.

I mean, you're a boy. You know how they are, right?

ROGER: I do.

TRACY: I feel their eyeballs burrowing through my clothes and going deeper, deeper, deeper until they're looking through my skin, through my fat, my muscles. Until they're looking at the deepest part of me. Then when their eyes hit my heart, I feel my heart stop.

Why do they do it?

Can you tell me?

ROGER: I don't know.

TRACY: I want to be good.

I want to be nice.

I want to be kind.

The saddest thing is I've done those things under the bleachers now. Not with Justin Dellarosa. Other boys. The feelings I'm feeling, they don't belong to me anymore. Those people I tried to be kind to? Those people who wanted me to be someone else? They're in control now. They've made me this contemptible thing. I don't know where the good is anymore, I don't know how to be one of the nice ones. Just let me go home.

> *She crawls under the conference table. Like a kid who doesn't want to be seen anymore. It's awkward and sad.*
>
> *Roger kneels down so she can see him. Looks at her with compassion.*

ROGER (*genuine*): I'm sorry.

TRACY: Why?

ROGER: I'm just sorry the other kids make you feel that way. My name's Roger.

TRACY: Hi Roger.

> *He offers her a Kleenex.*

ROGER: Listen, I'm gonna say something that probably won't make sense to you right now.

TRACY: Okay.

ROGER: If you ever feel like you have to do something drastic to yourself—to your body—so that you can feel like you're in control again...don't do it. You're perfect, just the way you are.

TRACY: Thank you.

ROGER: And you should know that I'm not one of those boys who tries to look inside you. I'm one of the good guys, okay?

TRACY: Okay.

ROGER: And if that woman who was in here before—

TRACY: Wanda?

ROGER: Yes, Wanda. She's going to ask you questions. But you should know she's one of the Elizabeth Hernandezes of the world. She'll try to use you. She'll try to turn you against me. And if she does that, just tell her I'm a good guy. Because I'm going to help you.

TRACY: Okay.

Thank you.

Tracy crawls back out from under the table.

Beat. Switch.

TRACY: Roger?

Did you feel for me when I told you that story just now? Did you have empathy?

ROGER: *What*?

TRACY: I ask because your wife has a story like that. One of these days your daughter will have a story like that too. If you want me to keep you out of the shitstorm that's about to take place at Tender Forms Weight Loss Systems, I'd advise you to go home and be a better man.

ROGER: Tracy—

TRACY: No. Stop talking. You talk enough. Try to be better. *Just try.* Your default seems to be "privileged misogynistic fuckwit," so stop listening to your instincts. It won't be easy and you'll probably fail, but maybe—just maybe—you'll be better than you are now. That's all we can hope for. Will you try to do that? Because if you try, then I'll try to keep you out of the mess that's coming.

> *He nods, taking in her words. Actually hearing her.*

ROGER: Okay.

TRACY: Okay what?

ROGER: I'll try.

TRACY: Good. You can leave now.

ROGER: Can I just say one more thing?

TRACY: No.

He gets the message. Exits.

After a beat, Tracy laughs. It's a surprised laugh. Like a little girl who can't believe she got away with something.

But then her face fills with pain. She lets her aggression out on her legs, rubbing them, pawing at them, trying to will them away.

A quick beat as she composes herself, then:

Neal comes back in with a glass of water.

Wanda follows him in with the aspirin. Tracy immediately shifts back into teen mode. Neal hands her the water.

TRACY: What took you so long?
NEAL: It was a whole thing.
WANDA (*handing the pills to Tracy*): Here. Hopefully this will help your head.
TRACY: I want to go home. You don't mind taking me home, do you?

WANDA: I don't mind. But we're going to swing by the hospital first.

TRACY: Will my mom be there?

WANDA: Don't worry about that now.

    I need you to relax.

    Take a deep breath.

    And exhale.

Beat.

    Good.

    Are you feeling any better yet?

TRACY: Yes. My mom's not going to like whatever happened to me here. And you should know she isn't afraid to sue.

A beat.

Tracy lets herself feel the victory.

This thing she's been fighting for, hoping for, desperate for: it's finally within her grasp. She's going to get the procedure she needs.

She is flooded with relief, with hope.

*The fight, the struggle,
it's almost over.*

*Tears fill her eyes as she feels
the joy
of letting go.*

She's about to be a complete person.

She's about to be whole.

TRACY: I can't feel my legs. *I can't feel my legs.*

Lights out.

END OF PLAY

About the Playwright

ERIK PATTERSON is an award-winning playwright, screenwriter, and writing teacher.

His play, *One of the Nice Ones*, earned the Los Angeles Drama Critics Circle Award. His theater work has been produced or developed by Playwrights' Arena, the Los Angeles Theatre Centre, Theatre of NOTE, the Evidence Room, The Actors' Gang, the Echo Theater Company, the Lark Play Development Center, Moving Arts, Black Dahlia, Naked Angels, the Mark Taper Forum, and New Group. His plays have been nominated for the Ovation Award, the Stage Raw Award, the LA Weekly Award, and the GLAAD Media Award.

His writing for TV has been recognized with the Humanitas Prize and the Writer's Guild Award, as well as two Emmy nominations. Along with his writing partner, Jessica Scott, Erik has written films for Warner Bros., Universal, 20th Century Fox, Disney, Freeform, MTV, Paramount, Hallmark, and Syfy, among others. Film and TV credits include: *Abandoned* (starring Emma Roberts and Michael Shannon), *R.L. Stine's The Haunting Hour*, *Another Cinderella Story* (starring Selena Gomez and Jane Lynch), *Deep Blue Sea 2*, *Radio Rebel*, and many more.

Erik is a graduate of Occidental College and the British American Drama Academy. He hosts a gently-guided writing sprint online called "Sunday Sprints" that attracts writers seeking community and inspiration to do their best work.

www.erikpatterson.org

Plays by Erik Patterson

Tonseisha
drama / 1 female, 5 male / 45 minutes, no intermission
A young Japanese woman is haunted by the loss of two men: her father, whom she barely knew, and cult novelist Richard Brautigan, whom she never met. Akiko plays out her father/Richard Brautigan fantasies with a new man nearly every night. Each one of her relationships begins in a bar and ends in a bedroom, and she's never satisfied. She's so lost...can she ever be found?

Yellow Flesh / Alabaster Rose
dark comedy / 5 female, 4 male / full length, one intermission
Elliot is lost in a world of sex workers—late night house calls from hustlers and phone calls with call girls. Becky is torn between two worlds—her day job as a stripper and being a mom to fifteen-year-old Rose (a Goth girl who wants nothing to do with her). And then there's Little B, who has stripped away every piece of herself until all she has left is her obsession with Icelandic pop singer Bjork. This troubled family's shared past holds unspeakable horrors and they must join forces if they ever want to heal. *Winner of the Backstage West Garland Award for Best Playwriting.*

Red Light, Green Light
drama / 6 female, 7 male / full length, one intermission
A gay clown. Two lesbian strippers. A pregnant Goth teen. A deadbeat dad. A horny mother. And a girl who thinks she's Bjork. In this stand-alone sequel to *Yellow Flesh / Alabaster Rose*, the Silverstein family journey towards healing is abruptly halted when Elliot becomes the victim of a brutal gay bashing.

He Asked For It
drama / 1 female, 6 male / full length, one intermission
It's the early 2000s, before PrEP. Ted is new to Los Angeles, and newly out of the closet. He goes on a journey through Hollywood back rooms, nightclub bathrooms, and Internet chat rooms—where he meets and falls in love with Henry. But Henry doesn't yet know how to navigate the dating landscape with his new HIV diagnosis, so he breaks things off with Ted...who then makes a desperate decision to win Henry back. *He Asked For It* asks how far are you willing to go for love? And how much will you forgive? *GLAAD Media Award nominee for Outstanding Los Angeles Theater.*

Sick
dramedy / 3 female, 3 male, 1 child / full length, no intermission
David needs to get laid, Gary could use a drink, and Tim would like you to take your top off. Carla craves cocaine, Jeannie's got God, and Pamela keeps digging herself deeper into the funny and frightening world of hypochondria. But when one of their own gets sick for real, they're all going to have to face their greatest fears and grow up.

I Wanna Hold Your Hand
dramedy / 3 female, 3 male / full length, no intermission
Our lives can change in an instant. One moment you're getting engaged, and a few surreal moments later you're sitting with strangers in an ICU waiting room, praying your fiancé will survive a brain aneurysm. While waiting for Frank to wake from a coma, Ada meets Julia, Paul, and Josh, who are waiting for their mom to wake up. A tenuous friendship is born. *I Wanna Hold Your Hand* looks at life, death, and recovery, and what it means to try your hand at living again...

One of the Nice Ones
dark comedy / 2 female, 2 male / 90 minutes, no intermission
A paraplegic woman plays outrageous power games to get something she desperately wants in this dark, twisty, sexy play that takes office politics to new extremes. *Winner of the Los Angeles Drama Critics Circle Award for Best Playwriting.*

Handjob
dark comedy / 2 female, 4 male / 90 minutes, no intermission
An encounter between a white, gay playwright and his black, straight "shirtless maid" goes disastrously wrong when signals are misinterpreted, lines crossed. *Handjob* explores the aftermath of their meeting, as it reveals deep layers of discrimination, discord, and discontent among people who should be allies. How do you know when you've gone too far if you completely ignore other people's boundaries?

Books by Erik Patterson

Pop Prompts: 200 Writing Prompts Inspired by Popular Music
Available on Amazon and the TikTok Shop in paperback and e-book

Pop Prompts is a collection of writing prompts that will help you dig deeper and break through creative blocks. Each prompt is paired with a pop song. Let the music be your muse as you work on your memoir, novel, script, poem—or even your own songs. This book can also be a daily jumpstart for therapeutic journaling. Use it however you want, whenever you want. As long as you're writing you're doing it right.

Pop Prompts For Swifties: 99 Writing Prompts
Available on Amazon and the TikTok Shop in paperback and e-book

Every writing prompt in this book is paired with one of Taylor's songs from the first "era" of her storytelling journey, from her debut album *Taylor Swift* (2006), to *Fearless* (2008), to *Speak Now* (2010), to *Red* (2012), and all the way through *1989* (2014). You don't even have to be a Swiftie—anyone can use these prompts for self-expression and reflection. As a bonus, each prompt includes blank journal pages. Inspiration is only a song away. Put on your favorite Taylor Swift album, pick a prompt, and start writing! Taylor Swift has no involvement in this book. The use of her name is merely descriptive and should not be interpreted as a sign of endorsement.

Pop Prompts: The '90s
Available on Amazon and the TikTok Shop in paperback and e-book

Pop Prompts: The '90s takes you on a journey through a decade of music that will liberate the writer in you from whatever holds you back. R&B, rock, rap, grunge, hip-hop, pop, punk. The lines between genres and mainstream vs. counterculture music often disappeared as '90s musicians embraced the mantra of their time: anything goes. Now it's your turn. Each '90s song in this book is your cue to write with abandon.

Pop Prompts Showtunes
Available on Amazon and the TikTok Shop in paperback and e-book

Pop Prompts Showtunes is organized by different types of musical theater song, from the "Opening Number" to "I Want" songs to the "11 O'Clock Number" all the way through the big Finale. Every showtunes is accompanied by four writing prompts. Depending on what you're writing, you'll follow a different path through the book: Musical Prompts, Fiction Prompts, Journaling Prompts, and Stagecraft Prompts. The book ends with a Master Class, which looks closely at the musical *Fun Home*, taking inspiration from each and every song.

SUNDAY SPRINTS

Need some motivation?

Do you work better when someone is holding you accountable?

Come to SUNDAY SPRINTS.

Erik Patterson hosts gently-guided writing sprints on Zoom every Wednesday from 6 to 8 p.m. PST and every Sunday from noon to 2 p.m. PST. (Yes, it's called Sunday Sprints on Wednesdays because... why not?)

Here's how it works: I give a new writing prompt every fifteen minutes. You write. That's it.

All sprinters stay on mute. Alone but not alone, you can draw creative energy from the community of writers on your screen. This is a fun, low-pressure environment—a safe space for you to experiment with your writing. No worries: I will never ask you to share your work.

You decide how to use this distraction-free writing time. Work on that screenplay, novel, short story, play, poem, song. Do some therapeutic journaling. Write letters to loved ones. Do some technical writing. Create a D&D campaign. Finish your homework. Seriously, whatever you need to work on.

Let's get that writing done. Together.

Join the Sunday Sprints Patreon at:
www.patreon.com/erikpatterson

Subscribe to the Sunday Sprints mailing list at:
www.erikpatterson.org/sundaysprints

www.ingramcontent.com/pod-product-compliance
Lightning Source LLC
Chambersburg PA
CBHW050208130526
44590CB00043B/3263